Treasure!

Written by Elizabeth Sengel

Illustrated by Gioia Fiammenghi

STECK-VAUGHN
COMPANY

A Division of Harcourt Brace & Company

Dean and Jeanie went to see Grandma Mead in her big old house. They had not seen her for a long time. They were really excited.

2

"Follow the leader," Grandma said when they went in the house. "I have a treat for you in the kitchen."

3

Grandma set out bowls of ice cream. Then she put peaches on top. "You have not been here since you were little," Grandma said. "Why don't you have a look around when you finish eating?"

4

Dean and Jeanie smiled. They ate their ice cream and helped Grandma clean up. Then they raced each other up the stairs. "What a neat old house!" said Jeanie.

5

Dean and Jeanie opened a heavy door. It creaked. When they poked their heads in the room, they saw heaps of old things. They held their breath and tiptoed inside.

Jeanie found an old hat with a feather.
Dean put on a huge sweater and a cowboy
hat. Jeanie teased him. "That hat is way too
big for your head!" she said.

7

Grandma came in. "Do you want to see some old pictures?" she asked. She took a seat on the trunk and opened a photo album. Dean and Jeanie leaned over to look. A sheet of paper slid out of the album.

8

"It's a treasure map! This could mean there's treasure on your land," said Jeanie. "Please, may we look for it?"

"It's nearly dark outside," said Grandma. "You can look for it tomorrow instead."

9

The next morning Dean and Jeanie raced down to the kitchen. Grandma was cooking breakfast. "Eat a healthy meal before you leave," she said. "Treasure hunting is really hard work!"

Jeanie read the map. "First we go west toward the bridge. Then we cut across East Meadow to the big tree. Ready? This will be easy!"

Dean said, "Here's the big tree." They dug until they felt something.

"Heave, ho!" he said and lifted out a box.

"It's the treasure!" Jeanie squealed.

Dean and Jeanie raced back to the house. Grandma was in the kitchen making bread. "You found the treasure!" she said. "Go ahead and open it."

13

A leather scrapbook and two five-dollar bills lay in the box. Jeanie reached for the scrapbook. "What is that?" asked Dean.

Grandma's eyes gleamed. "It's your father's scrapbook. He made it when he was a boy," she said. "It has his drawings and some leaves and feathers he found."

15

Jeanie looked at Grandma. "You made the map, didn't you?"

Grandma smiled. "Yes, I did. I hid the treasure, too. Now you each have a money treasure—and a family treasure!"